MW00773000

GALE
CENGAGE Learning

Novels for Students, Volume 29

Project Editor: Sara Constantakis Rights Acquisition and Management: Mollika Basu, Leitha Etheridge-Sims, Jacqueline Flowers, Barb McNeil Composition: Evi Abou-El-Seoud Manufacturing: Drew Kalasky

Imaging: John Watkins

Product Design: Pamela A. E. Galbreath, Jennifer Wahi Content Conversion: Civie Green, Katrina Coach Product Manager: Meggin Condino © 2009 Gale, Cengage Learning

For product information and technology assistance, contact us at **Gale Customer Support, 1-800-877-4253.**

For permission to use material from this text or product, submit all requests online at **www.cengage.com/permissions**.

Further permissions questions can be emailed to **permissionrequest@cengage.com** While every effort has been made to ensure the reliability of the information presented in this publication, Gale, a part of Cengage Learning, does not guarantee the accuracy of the data contained herein. Gale accepts no payment for listing; and inclusion in the publication of any organization, agency, institution, publication, service, or individual does not imply endorsement of the editors or publisher. Errors brought to the attention of the publisher and verified to the satisfaction of the publisher will be corrected in future editions.

Gale
27500 Drake Rd.
Farmington Hills, MI, 48331-3535

ISBN-13: 978-0-7876-8686-4
ISBN-10: 0-7876-8686-7
ISSN 1094-3552

This title is also available as an e-book.
ISBN-13: 978-1-4144-4945-6
ISBN-10: 1-4144-4945-3
Contact your Gale, a part of Cengage Learning sales
representative for ordering information.

Printed in the United States of America
1 2 3 4 5 6 7 13 12 11 10 09

Something Wicked This Way Comes

Ray Bradbury 1962

Introduction

Published in 1962, *Something Wicked This Way Comes*, by Ray Bradbury, is arguably the last of the author's most beloved novels. It was written on the heels of his science-fiction classics *The Martian Chronicles* and *Fahrenheit 451* as well as his widely read bildungsroman *Dandelion Wine*. In fact, *Something Wicked This Way Comes* combines elements of the bildungsroman (a coming-of-age story) with elements of science fiction. Appealing to children and adults alike, the story, which lies on the cusp between the horror and fantasy genres, portrays two boys and their adventures with a mystical circus and its sinister ringmaster. Ultimately a meditation on the power of love in the face of evil, the novel contains a wealth of themes, ranging from the natures of transformation to the graceful acceptance of aging. By virtue of the story's considerable thematic depth, coupled with its plethora of fantastical imagery and its accessibility to younger readers, the book has been a mainstay in school curricula, kept there for several decades by the timeless nature of the novel's themes and content. *Something Wicked This Way Comes* has been more or less continuously in print since 1962; a relatively recent edition of the novel was printed by Eos in 1999.

Author Biography

Ray Bradbury was born on August 22, 1920, in Waukegan, Illinois. He was the third son of Spaulding Bradbury (a telephone lineman) and Esther Marie Moberg Bradbury (a Swedish immigrant). A reader from an early age, Bradbury spent a great deal of time in the Waukegan town library, upon which the library in *Something Wicked This Way Comes* is based. Bradbury began writing around the age of twelve. On his personal Web site, Bradbury reports that he was inspired to become a writer after attending a carnival where a man performing as Mr. Electrico touched him with a sword and told him, "Live forever." (A character based on Mr. Electrico also appears in *Something Wicked This Way Comes*.) Though Bradbury's hometown is Waukegan, the family often moved as Spaulding Bradbury looked for jobs during the Great Depression. The family finally settled in Los Angeles in 1934.

Bradbury graduated from Los Angeles High School in 1938, at which time he chose to forgo college and immediately begin his writing career. That year, he published his first short story, "Hollerbochen's Dilemma." The following year, he founded his own magazine, *Futuria Fantasia*. In 1942, Bradbury wrote "The Lake," the first of his stories to exhibit the style for which he would ultimately become famous. By the mid-1940s his work was being published in more prominent publications; his "The Big Black and White Game" appeared in *Best American Short Stories 1945*, and his "I See You Never" appeared in *Best American Short Stories 1948*. He also received recognition from the O. Henry Award organization for two consecutive years, publishing "Homecoming" in the *O. Henry Prize Stories 1947* and winning the O. Henry Award in 1948 for "Powerhouse." On September 27, 1947, Bradbury married Marguerite Susan McClure. The couple had four daughters, Susan Marguerite, Ramona, Bettina, and Alexandra. After over fifty-five years of marriage, Marguerite passed away in 2003.

In 1950, Bradbury achieved his first major success with the novel (or collection of linked short stories) *The Martian Chronicles*. The book was an instant classic that would be adapted as a play (by Bradbury) and also as a movie. Indeed, several of Bradbury's best works underwent dramatic adaptations, often written by Bradbury himself. Bradbury's next major work, the novel *Fahrenheit 451* (1953), was also a success and became a dystopian classic. Based on the merits of these early works alone, Bradbury received the National Institute of Arts and Letters Award for his contributions to American literature in 1954. The autobiographical *Dandelion Wine* followed in 1957, and *Something Wicked This Way Comes* was published in 1962. The latter draws heavily upon stories from Bradbury's early collections *Dark Carnival* (1947) and *The Illustrated Man* (1951). That latter book's title story, "The Illustrated Man," is perhaps one of Bradbury's most anthologized works.

Although Bradbury never again matched his early successes, he has remained a prolific writer well into his late eighties. He is the author of novels, short stories, children's books and stories, poems, plays, and screenplays. His unique work has defied easy categorization, containing elements of fantasy, horror, science fiction, gothic writing, and autobiographical fiction. Given this, critics initially debated the merits of Bradbury's writing, and he did not receive much critical recognition until later in his career. For this reason, the bulk of Bradbury's honors have come more than forty years after the release of his best works. His later awards have mostly been given for his oeuvre as a whole rather than for individual books or collections. Bradbury earned the PEN Body of Work Award in 1985, a 2000 medal for "Distinguished Contribution to American Letters" from the National Book Foundation, a star on the Hollywood Walk of Fame for his screenplays, a 2004 National Medal of Arts; a special citation for a distinguished career from the Pulitzer Board in 2007, and a 2007 Commandeur medal from the French Ordre des Arts et des Lettres. As of 2008, Bradbury was living in Los Angeles, continuing to write every day, just as he had since he was twelve years old.

Prologue

It is October 23. The next-door neighbors and best friends James (Jim) Nightshade and William (Will) Halloway are each about to turn fourteen, William on October 30 and James on October 31. Their lives, however, are about to change, for this is the "week when they grew up overnight."

I. Arrivals

CHAPTERS 1-5

Jim and Will are playing in front of their houses when a lightning rod salesman walks by. The salesman, Tom Fury, wants to sell them a rod, but the boys have no money and their parents are not home. Tom Fury suddenly has a premonition that Jim's house will be catastrophically struck by lightning that very night, so he gives the boys a lightning rod for free. Later that evening, Jim and Will run to the library. On the way there, Jim thinks he hears faint music, but Will does not hear it, and Jim thinks he must have been mistaken. Will's father, Charles William Halloway, is the janitor at the library. He looks so old to Will that it is hard for him to see his father as his dad and not as an old man.

Charles watches the boys leaving the library

with their books, running. He wishes he could join them and be young again. Charles finishes up at the library and stops at the local bar for a nightcap. Meanwhile, the boys reach the United Cigar Store and greet Mr. Tetley, the store's owner. Mr. Tetley greets the boys, but then he suddenly stares off into space, listening for something. The boys attempt to get his attention but fail, so they leave him standing there and keep running. They then come across the barber, Mr. Crosetti, as he closes up the barber shop. The barber thinks he smells cotton candy. Later, as Charles leaves the bar, he sees a man in a "dark suit" putting up posters; he enters and then exits an empty store before leaving. Charles looks into the storefront and sees a sign advertising Cooger & Dark's Pandemonium Shadow Show, along with a display claiming to contain "THE MOST BEAUTIFUL WOMAN IN THE WORLD." All that is there is an empty block of ice.

CHAPTERS 6-10

Jim and Will continue on their way home when Jim wants to stop and look at the Theater, which is not a real theater but a house with an uncovered window that the boys peep into. Will refuses to go with Jim, so Jim goes without him, calling Will a "dimwit Episcopal Baptist." However, Jim soon catches back up with Will since no one is at the Theater. Apiece of paper goes flying by in the wind, and it turns out to be a poster for Cooger & Dark's Pandemonium Shadow Show, which is scheduled to begin the next day. Will is suspicious and says that there are never any carnivals in the fall. Jim is nevertheless excited. The boys realize that the faint music and smells of cotton candy must be from the carnival. Will then points out that carnivals arrive at dawn, not at dusk. Soon, the boys reach their houses.

Will finds that his father has arrived home before him; his father and mother are in the living room. Will thinks that his mother always seems happy but his father always seems sad. Will goes to bed and listens to his parents talking. Charles says that he regrets being too old to play ball with his own son. Will's parents then go to bed. Just as Will is falling asleep, he thinks he hears his father leave the house, and he assumes that Charles is going back to the library, where he often goes to be alone or to read.

Jim is lying in bed. Jim's mother comes in to say good night, and she worries about him leaving the window open. She worries because Jim is her only surviving child, the other two presumably having died in infancy. She warns him that he will worry, too, once he has children, but Jim says, "No use making more people. People die." Jim asks his mother about his father; it is not clear if Jim's father has died or if he left Jim's mother.

Tom Fury walks through the town, his pack empty. He comes upon the storefront advertising the beautiful woman and, when he looks inside, sees far more than Charles Halloway did. He sees a literal woman. Tom Fury thinks that if he were to touch the ice it would melt and free the woman within, so he enters the shop.

Media Adaptations

- *Something Wicked This Way Comes* was adapted as a Disney film, directed by Jack Clayton, in 1983. Bradbury wrote the screenplay.

CHAPTERS 11-15

It is three o'clock in the morning, and Will and Jim hear the carnival train approaching the town. Jim decides to sneak out to watch the proceedings, and Will follows him. The train passes over the boys on the bridge, and they see that no one is playing the calliope (a steam-powered pipe organ) emitting the ghostly church music. The train stops in a meadow, and everything is still. Then a green hot-air balloon descends, seemingly from nowhere, and hovers over the train. A "shadow-faced" man in a "dark suit" exits the train and raises his arms.

Suddenly, everything springs into action, as people silently exit the train and begin to set up the circus tents. The silence is disconcerting, especially to Will, who realizes that the setting up of carnivals is usually a lively and noisy event. The balloon blocks the moonlight, and it becomes too dark to see what is going on. The tent poles are set up, and the canvas is about to be brought out when the boys "somehow" realize that "the wires high-flung on the poles were catching swift clouds, ripping them free from the wind in streamers which, stitched and sewn by some great monster shadow, made canvas and more canvas as the tent took shape." When the boys are able to see again, everything is still and the people have disappeared. Both Jim and Will are frightened, though Jim is also fascinated, and when they reach town, both boys run back to their houses on their own. From the library window, Charles sees the boys running home. He has also heard the strange music and the train's whistle.

The next morning, Will and Jim go to the carnival. In the sunlight, the tents and flags look normal, as does the train. The boys run into Miss Foley, their seventh-grade teacher. She is looking for her nephew Robert and decides to enter the Mirror Maze, since he may be in there. Will does not want her to go in, but she does. When Jim asks Will why he is afraid of the maze, Will replies that the mirrors are "the only things *like* last night." Indeed, Miss Foley is soon screaming for help, so the boys rush in, find her, and pull her from the maze. She has a bruise on her face from falling but is otherwise fine. She tells the boys that there was a girl trapped in the maze who looked like her when she was very young. Miss Foley forgets all about her nephew and decides to go home. Will wants to go home, too, but Jim says they are staying until dark so that they can find out more about the strange carnival. Will agrees, but they both decide they will not enter the Mirror Maze.

CHAPTERS 16-20

Throughout the day, Will and Jim enjoy themselves, going on rides and playing games. At dusk, Jim disappears, and Will finds him at the mouth of the Mirror Maze. Will drags Jim out of the maze and yells at him. Jim stands there in shock, trying (and failing) to tell Will what he has seen. Will decides that they are going home, and Jim makes him promise that they can come back later that night. As they leave the carnival, they trip over a large bag. The bag belongs to Tom Fury, and all of his lightning rods are in it. The boys realize that the storm he predicted did not come, but they cannot think of a reason why he would have left everything he owned behind. Jim insists that they go back to find out what happened to Tom Fury. Will resists; the place is almost empty, and everyone at the carnival has gone home. Nevertheless, the two boys reenter the carnival.

The boys inspect the broken carousel, the only ride they have not been on. A large man picks Jim up and yells at him for climbing on the broken ride; Will runs to Jim's aid, and the man picks Will up in his other hand. Another man comes out and tells the large man to put the boys down, introducing himself to the boys as Dark and the man who has just released them as Cooger. They are the proprietors of the carnival. Mr. Dark ignores Will and focuses on Jim, handing him a business card that continuously changes its appearance. It turns out that Mr. Dark is also the Illustrated Man, and he shows a fascinated Jim one of his tattoos, which appears to move. Jim tells Mr. Dark that his name is Simon. Mr. Dark then tells the boys to come back at seven o'clock, when the carnival reopens for the evening, and he gives Jim a ticket for a free carousel ride to use once the ride has been repaired. The boys pretend to leave, and Jim jumps into a nearby tree, pulling Will up after him.

The boys spy on Cooger and Dark as they begin to operate the carousel, which moves backwards. Even the carousel's calliope music is being played backwards. Mr. Cooger jumps onto the ride, and Will and Jim realize that he is growing a year younger with each revolution of the carousel. Jim counts each turn of the ride; when it stops, Mr. Cooger is about twelve years old. Will and Jim stare in disbelief. The boys are frightened, but they run off after Cooger to see what he will do.

As they follow Cooger, Will sees a sign in the barbershop, but he does not register whatever it says. Cooger has turned onto the street where Miss Foley lives, and Will and Jim pass by her house, only to see Cooger through her window. Will thinks that they must be mistaken and that the boy they are seeing is Miss Foley's nephew, but Jim says that the boy in the window and Mr. Cooger have the same eyes. He says, "That's one part of people don't change, young, old, six or sixty!" The boys go into the house and pretend they are checking on Miss Foley after the incident at the maze. She says she is fine and introduces them to her nephew, who is really Mr. Cooger. Will somehow knows that the imposter is "evil."

Will is about to tell Miss Foley what's going on, but then he suddenly realizes that the sign in the barbershop said "CLOSED ON ACCOUNT OF ILLNESS," so he instead tells her that Mr. Crosetti is dead. The imposter invites the boys to join them for dessert, as he and his aunt are going back to the carnival later that night. Will asks Miss Foley why she would want to go back after the incident at the maze, but she says she was just being silly. Will then says that they cannot come to dessert because Jim's mother is sick. As Will and Jim are leaving, Will desperately wants to tell Miss Foley not to go to the carnival. Outside Miss Foley's house, Will realizes that the backwards tune on the merry-go-round was Frederic Chopin's "Funeral March" (and that it played in reverse because the carousel was taking Cooger further from death).

The boys return to their respective homes, only to be yelled at for being late, and they are sent to bed without supper. At ten o'clock, Will's father unlocks the door. Without opening it, he tells Will to "be careful." Will wishes his father would come in and talk to him, but he does not. Will overhears his father tell his mother that he feels too old to bond with his son. Charles then leaves the house, presumably returning to the library. Will wonders about his father's advice to be careful. Does his father also sense that the carnival is not what it seems?

CHAPTERS 21-24

Will notices Jim sneaking out of his window, and he is clearly planning to go out without Will. Will decides to follow Jim, and they soon come to Miss Foley's house. Jim stands outside the house trying to get Cooger's attention. Will jumps out from the bushes and tries to stop Jim, but Jim will not listen, and Will realizes that Jim saw himself as an older man in the Mirror Maze and that Jim wants to become older by riding the carousel. Cooger sees the boys, throws Miss Foley's jewelry onto the lawn, and begins screaming for the police before running off down the road. Miss Foley looks out the window and suspects Will and Jim of having robbed her. Jim takes off after Cooger/Robert, and Will takes off after Jim. Will knows that he and Jim will be branded as thieves and that now no one will believe them when they tell them about the carnival.

Cooger runs toward the carnival and the carousel, starting it up and jumping on just ahead of the boys. The carousel is moving forward, and Will knows that Cooger will grow to become a man who can easily kill them. Then, Jim is about to jump onto the merry-go-round when Will catches up and wrestles him to the ground. The boys struggle over the carousel switch, pulling it back and forth. The carousel goes haywire, spinning Cooger around faster and faster, and then the control box explodes. On the carousel, which has now come to a stop, lies a shriveled old man who looks like a mummy. Cooger must now be almost 130 years old; he struggles for breath and seems as if he is about to die.

The boys run to a pay phone and call the police and an ambulance. They fear for Cooger's life. When the police cars and ambulances appear, the boys lead them to the carousel, but no one is there. The police are skeptical of the boys' story. As they call for Mr. Cooger, the sideshow tent opens, and they are invited in. Will sees a tiny dwarf playing cards and realizes that it is Tom Fury and that he has somehow been transformed into a small, gnarled creature. They see Mr. Cooger on an electric chair. Mr. Dark is there, naked from the waist up, tattooing himself. He welcomes the police and tells them that they are rehearsing a new act. Will insists that Mr. Cooger is dead (he thinks that he and Jim are responsible and that the carnival people will take their revenge out on them), but Dark says that Cooger is their new act, Mr. Electrico. Dark then electrocutes Cooger, who comes to life. The policemen laugh, and the medics look uncomfortable. Will is confused; he wants Cooger to live so that the carnival people will not want revenge, but at the same time, he thinks, "Even more I want him dead, I want them all dead, they scare me so much." Cooger tells the police that he pretended to be dead when he caught the boys spying on him. Mr. Dark offers everyone free passes. The boys give Mr. Dark fake names, grab the tickets, and rush off to the police car, waiting to be driven home.

II. Pursuits

CHAPTERS 25-29

Miss Foley is alone in her house. On her dresser, she has a ticket to ride the carousel. She senses that her nephew is not her nephew and that he tried to frame Jim and Will, but she does not care. From her window, she sees a light on in the library, and she calls there. Charles picks up the phone, and she asks him to meet her at the police station right away.

In the police car, one of the medics says he could swear that Mr. Electrico was really dead. The policemen laugh this off. The boys give the police the fake names they gave Mr. Dark and also give them fake addresses that are close to the police station. Alone, the boys discuss their suspicions of what might have become of Tom Fury, and Will begins to think that something could have happened to Mr. Crosetti at the carnival as well.

While Will has thrown his free tickets away, he notices that Jim has kept his. Will realizes that Jim is still thinking about riding the carousel to become older. The boys overhear voices coming from the police station, and they sneak under the window to eavesdrop. Miss Foley and Charles Halloway are conversing there, and Miss Foley is telling Charles about the robbery. Miss Foley says she does not want to press charges, but she also says, "If they are innocent, where are the boys?" Before Jim can stop him, Will says they are there, and he jumps through the window and into the police station.

Charles takes Will and Jim home. When Will and his father are alone, Charles tells his son that he is lucky Miss Foley is not going to prosecute; then he asks Will why he confessed. Charles knows his son well enough to know that since he is not acting guilty, he did not actually steal anything. Will tells his father that Miss Foley "*wants* us guilty" so that no one will believe what he and Jim say. He says they confessed anyway since the police would "go easy" on them, which they did. Charles does not understand, but Will promises his father that he will tell him what is going on "in a couple days." Will asks his father to stay away from the carnival. Charles tells his son that he was planning to say the same thing.

After going to bed, Will sleeps for about an hour. He hears a strange sound and looks out his window. In a few moments, the carnival's hot-air balloon appears. Jim sees it, too. One of the sideshow freaks, the Dust Witch, is inside. She appears to be a lifeless wax figure, though she is indeed alive. She is blind, but she is able to sense and smell souls. As she comes closer, she seems to find what she is looking for. She descends over Jim's house and leaves a mark on his roof, and then she floats away. As soon as she is gone, Jim and Will climb up to Jim's roof.

The boys remove the mark on the roof, but the balloon hovers on the horizon, and Will fears that the Dust Witch senses their plan. The boys go back to bed, but Will is unable to sleep. He sees his bow and arrow and has an idea. He begins sending excited thoughts out to the witch, letting her know that they have duped her, and he sees the balloon turn and head back in his direction. Will runs to an abandoned house nearby, luring the witch to the roof there. When she comes close, Will turns to shoot the arrow, but it breaks in his hands. The witch begins to raise the balloon, but Will grabs hold of the basket and throws the arrowhead. The arrowhead hits its mark, and the balloon begins to lurch wildly as it loses air. Will is thrown to the roof, tumbling off and landing safely in a tree. The balloon jerks away and appears to be heading back toward the carnival.

The rest of the night is uneventful, and by sunrise it is raining. Over the noise of the storm, only Miss Foley hears the carousel start up again. She sets out for the carnival, walking through the then-deserted town. Later that morning, Will and Jim set off to the police station, where they will give their statements and then leave for Miss Foley's house so that they can apologize to her. Will tries to tell Jim about what happened with the balloon and the Dust Witch, but he does not get a chance because they are interrupted when they hear a little girl crying nearby.

They go to see the little girl and realize that it

is Miss Foley. The girl asks them to help her and says that no one will believe what has happened to her. Will tells her that he believes her but that he has to be sure, so the boys leave the little girl where she is and run back to Miss Foley's house. No one is there. The boys realize that the carousel must be working again, and as they head back for the transformed Miss Foley, they hear a band playing, and they know that the carnival is parading through town. The boys also know that the parade is only a ruse and that the carnival freaks are looking for the boys or Miss Foley or all three. When they get back to where they left Miss Foley, she is gone. Will and Jim run off to hide until the parade has left the town.

Later, Jim and Will are hiding under a grate in the sidewalk in front of the cigar store. It is a busy area of town, and crowds of people leaving church linger as the parade comes closer. The freaks' eyes search the crowd as they disperse and begin handing out flyers. Will sees his father walk by overhead.

CHAPTERS 35-39

The Dwarf, the transformed Tom Fury, stands near the grate. The Dwarf looks down and stares for a few moments, but he does not seem to see the boys. He continues walking, and the boys breathe a sigh of relief. Meanwhile, Charles Halloway is sitting in a nearby coffee shop when the Illustrated Man (Mr. Dark) walks in. The Illustrated Man says that he is "looking for two boys." Charles replies, "Who *isn't*?" before getting up and leaving the coffee shop. The Illustrated Man watches Charles leave, staring after him.

Not sure of where to go, Charles wanders over to the cigar shop and purchases a cigar. He lights it and drops the cigar wrapper down the grate. He glances down and sees Jim and Will. He starts to ask them what is going on just as the Illustrated Man leaves the coffee shop and starts walking toward him. Jim tells Charles that they will be found if Charles does not look up, explaining that the Illustrated Man is after them. Charles looks up and pretends to be checking his watch against the town's clock tower as the Illustrated Man approaches. Mr. Dark tells Charles that he is looking for two boys who have won unlimited free rides and candy, showing him a tattooed image of Will on the palm of one hand and a tattooed image of Jim on the other. Charles tries to hide his shock and gives him fake names for the boys. Mr. Dark says that he already knows the boys are named Will and Jim, but it is clear that he does not know their last names. Charles comments that there must be about two hundred boys in town with those names. Mr. Dark finally gives up and walks away.

Suddenly, the Dust Witch appears, bruised from her ordeal the night before. She is using her senses in an attempt to find the boys, and it seems as if she has become aware of Will and Jim's proximity. She moves toward Charles Halloway, and Mr. Dark begins walking back toward him as well. Charles, however, suddenly comments on the high quality of his cigar, and he blows cigar smoke at the Dust Witch, distracting her and making her cough. Mr. Dark tries to stop Charles, so Charles buys him a cigar as well and continues to blow smoke at the witch. Mr. Dark asks Charles for his name, and Charles gives it willingly, telling him that he works at the library and that Mr. Dark should come to visit him there. Will is shocked at his father's bravery. Mr. Dark and the Dust Witch leave, unable to search in the midst of the cigar smoke. After they have gone, Charles pretends to talk to the clock tower, telling the boys to stay hidden for a couple of days. He says he will go to the library to research the carnival and find out whatever he can. They all agree to meet at the library at seven.

At seven, Charles waits at the library. Earlier in the day, he walked through the parade looking at the freaks. He then went to the carnival and made sure to stay out of the tents and away from the rides. He saw the Mirror Maze and was filled with foreboding. At the library, Charles has researched texts on the supernatural, on enchanted mirrors, and on the witching hours, from midnight to dawn. He waits for the boys to appear and wonders if they will be able to make it. The boys finally appear at a quarter to eight. They have been hiding in different places all over town and waiting for the sun to go down. They tell Charles everything that has happened. Charles believes them, and he shows them the old carnival flyers that he has found, dating back to the 1800s. The very same carnival comes every few decades, but only in October. The boys say that it cannot logically be the same Cooger and Dark each time, but their instincts tell them otherwise.

CHAPTERS 40-44

Charles realizes that the people who become younger or older on the carousel are filled with guilt and regret because they have left everything and everyone they know and love behind. He suspects that the carnival exploits their regret, making its victims work for it in exchange for returning them to their correct age. The freaks, Charles says, are people who have become symbolic physical manifestations of their sins. As he and the boys are trying to decide what to do about the carnival, they hear the library door open and close. Charles tells the boys to hide, and he sits and waits for whoever has just entered.

Mr. Dark reintroduces himself to Charles and asks where the boys are. He explains that the Dust Witch can make Charles's heart fail and that it will appear to be a natural death. Mr. Dark begins walking down the aisles of the library and calling for the boys. He tries to tempt Jim with a ride, saying that if Jim comes out and gives Will to him, then Jim can reap the rewards. Charles sits, feeling faint, but he resolves to get up if Mr. Dark finds the boys. The Illustrated Man changes tactics, telling Will that they have turned his mother into a two-hundred-year-old hag. Mr. Dark hears a sob and heads in the direction of the sound, climbing the shelves until he finds both boys huddled together at the top.

Mr. Dark grabs the boys, and they all tumble to the ground. Charles jumps out of the aisle and attempts to stop them, but Mr. Dark grasps Charles's hand and crushes it. Charles falls to the ground in agony. The boys continue to scream and struggle as Dark drags them toward the exit, but then the Dust Witch and some of the other freaks appear. The Dust Witch casts a spell on the boys that makes them unable to see, hear, or speak. Dark then tells the witch to take care of Charles.

The witch begins casting a spell to stop Charles's heart. His heart begins to slow, and he feels like giving in, like falling asleep. As he watches the witch's fingers move, as if they are "tickling" the air, the whole episode suddenly strikes Charles as hilarious. He begins to laugh, which upsets the witch. She attempts to keep casting her spell, but as Charles continues to giggle she is rendered powerless, and she runs from the library.

III. Departures

CHAPTERS 45-49

Dark marches the boys, who are unable to speak or move of their own volition, toward the carnival. He places the boys in the waxworks, which is located behind the Mirror Maze. To the crowd, Will and Jim appear to be wax figures. The Dust Witch returns, and Mr. Dark grabs her, announcing to the crowd that she will perform an act in which she is to be fired at by a rifle. As he asks for volunteers, Mr. Dark asks the witch if

Charles is dead, but the witch shakes her head. Mr. Dark is furious. When he turns back to face the crowd, Charles Halloway steps forward as a volunteer.

The crowd cheers for Charles. Mr. Dark tells Charles that he cannot possibly shoot with his injured hand, but Charles assures him that he can, and the crowd cheers again. Charles says that he will need a boy to volunteer as his other hand. He says that his son Will is in the crowd and can be his assistant. Charles begins calling for Will. Nothing happens. He keeps calling, and even the crowd joins in. Eventually, Will, still in a daze, appears and goes toward his father.

Dark hands Charles a bullet and tells him to mark it with his initials. Charles says that he will mark it with something better and carves a crescent moon into the bullet. The gun and bullet are handed back to Dark, who appears to load the gun. Dark, however, has passed the bullet to the witch, who will hide it in her mouth and pretend to have caught it in her teeth once the rifle has been fired. Dark places a blank in the rifle and hands it back to Charles. Charles opens the rifle, inspects the bullet, pretends not to notice that it has been switched, and then says that he would like to make his mark a little clearer. He carves the fake bullet with the same symbol as before. Mr. Dark is unperturbed by this.

Charles steadies the rifle over Will's shoulder. Dark then clenches his fist around the tattoo of Will's face, and Will, still in a fog, shudders, causing the rifle to fall. Charles replaces the rifle as if nothing has happened and cracks a joke to the crowd, and the crowd's laughter revives Will. Despite Mr. Dark's continued attempts to harm Will through the tattoo, Will is no longer affected amid the crowd's laughter. As Charles prepares to shoot, he whispers to the witch that the crescent moon on the two bullets is not actually a moon but is his own smile. Charles fires the gun.

The witch falls down dead, but Mr. Dark tells the crowd that she has fainted and that this is part of the show. Dark then tells the crowd that the show is over and the carnival is closing for the night. Charles tells Will to come with him, and they begin to run toward the Mirror Maze in order to retrieve Jim from the waxworks. Will is slowly coming out of his daze, as is Jim, though Jim is still unable to move. In the maze, Will and his father can see all of the lost souls that the carnival has claimed. A much older version of Charles also appears. Then, the lights in the Mirror Maze go out, and all is dark.

Will grabs kitchen matches from his pocket, just as it feels as if the infinite army of Charles's ancient reflections is closing in on them. Charles lights the match, but he begins to falter in the face of his old age. Will snaps him out of it, telling his father that he loves him no matter his age. Charles remembers himself, and he begins to laugh.

CHAPTERS 50-54

At the sound of Charles's laughter, the mirrors shatter. Jim, who is finally able to move, runs out the back of the tent. When Will and his father get to the waxworks, Jim is gone. Will and Charles can hear the carousel's music, and Will thinks Jim might be headed there, perhaps still wanting to grow older after all that has happened. The moon is starting to rise, and Will and his father are able to see by the moonlight. Will is worried about all of the sideshow freaks coming after them, but Charles tells his son that all they need to do is save Jim and get rid of Cooger and Dark. He says that if they get rid of the carnival masters, then the sideshow performers will go with them.

Will can see the sparks from Cooger/Mr. Electrico's electric chair, and he thinks that they are moving him to the carousel. Will wonders whose side Jim will be on in the final showdown between Dark, himself, and his father. The freaks stand motionless throughout the fairgrounds, and Charles thinks that this is because they are afraid of what happened to the witch; Will thinks it is because they are waiting for Dark's command to attack. Will realizes that the carousel music had been playing backward, but now it is playing forward.

Will and Charles come around a tent to find that Dark is nowhere to be found and that the ancient Cooger has finally expired into dust flakes; a heap of ash is all that remains in his chair. They see Jim running toward the carousel. Will chases after him but is unable to stop him. Jim jumps onto the ride but leaves one hand stretched out toward Will. Will attempts to grab Jim's hand, but to no avail, while Jim appears as if he wants to both jump from and stay on the carousel. Once Jim has gone around a few times, he looks back at Will as if he barely remembers him. Will grabs Jim's hand, with Jim on the ride and Will running beside him on the ground. Will's hand grows one year older while the rest of him stays the same age. Will tries to pull Jim from the carousel, but Jim is stronger, and Will is instead pulled onto the ride. Will then grabs Jim's arm and leaps from the ride. Jim is physically torn between Will's leap and the carousel pole he is grasping, and he cries out in pain, tumbling, unconscious, to the ground. Charles shuts the ride down, and Will wonders if Jim is dead.

Charles tells Will to give Jim "artificial respiration" as a small boy comes running from the carnival screaming that the man with the tattoos is after him. The boy says his name is Jed. Charles follows the boy, but he realizes that it is really Mr. Dark trying to trick him. Charles holds the boy close in a fond embrace, and the boy cries out that he is being murdered, that Charles is evil. Charles laughs, which only hurts the boy further, and says, "Good to evil seems evil. So I will do only good to you, Jed." Charles says that he will let the boy go if he tells him how to cure Jim. Dark refuses, and Charles continues to hold him lovingly. The boy's eyes grow dim, and he falls to the ground dead.

The freaks stand about moaning and disoriented, gathering around Will and Charles as they attempt to revive Jim. The tattoos on Dark's body shudder and begin to disappear, as if they, too, are dying. As the tattoos fade, the freaks are freed, and they run from the carnival, knocking over the tents as they go. One of the freaks picks up Dark's tiny body and walks away. Will thinks of all the carnival's victims: Dark, Cooger, Miss Foley, Tom Fury, and Mr. Crosetti. Then he turns back to Jim, but Jim's body is cold.

Will begins to cry, but Charles tells him that the only way to save Jim's life is to laugh. Will is skeptical, but Charles reminds him of how the mirrors were shattered by laughter and how the witch was killed by a smile. Charles forces Will to begin dancing, laughing, and singing. As the two dance about, they think that Jim looks a bit better, but Charles tells Will not to look and to keep dancing. Jim wakes and joins in the gaiety.

Charles says that the fight is never over, that there will always be people like those from the carnival, that they appear in many guises, and that he and the boys must always be on the lookout. Charles takes a wrench and smashes the carousel's machinery to pieces. The boys race home, and Charles joins in, too.

Characters

Mr. Cooger

Mr. Cooger is the less prominent of the evil carnival masters, though he is the first to come to Will and Jim's attention. The first night of the carnival, Jim and Will spy on Mr. Cooger as he transforms himself on the carousel into a young boy. As a young boy, Cooger masquerades as Robert, Miss Foley's nephew. When Cooger-as-Robert goes back to the carousel to return to his original age, Will and Jim accidentally cause the ride to malfunction, and Cooger becomes an ancient, near-dead mummy. In order to hide the transformation, the carnival masquerades the ancient Cooger as Mr. Electrico. At the end of the story, he finally expires, leaving nothing but dust behind.

Mr. Crosetti

Mr. Crosetti is the town barber. The boys run into him just before the carnival arrives in town. There is a faint smell of cotton candy in the air, and it makes the barber cry for the joys of his lost youth. The next day, there is a sign in the barbershop window that says the store has been closed on account of illness. The boys believe that Mr. Crosetti has become one of the carnival's victims.

Mr. Dark

The more evil and prominent of the two carnival masters, Mr. Dark goes after Jim and Will. Once he captures them, he commands the Dust Witch to turn them into automatons. Mr. Dark also attacks Will's father and has the Dust Witch attempt to kill him. At first, Mr. Dark is assured of his victory over Charles and the boys; he laughs at Charles's Bible, throwing it in the wastebasket. However, once Charles learns how to conquer evil, Mr. Dark avoids further confrontation with Charles. Instead, he tries to pass himself off as a small boy named Jed, claiming that he is being pursued by Mr. Dark. Charles is not fooled, and he literally kills the transformed Mr. Dark with kindness, holding him in a long embrace until he falls down dead.

Mr. Dark is also the Illustrated Man, and his tattoos have mystical properties. They appear to move of their own volition, and they also appear to be effigies of the sideshow freaks. Dark is able to control the freaks via these illustrations. For instance, he pinches a tattoo of a nun, and the Dust Witch writhes in agony. After Mr. Dark dies, his tattoos disappear, and the freaks are finally free.

Dust Witch

The most powerful sideshow performer, the Dust Witch is blind but has the ability to sense souls. She is sent to find Will and Jim in a hot-air balloon. When she finds Jim's house, she marks the roof with a silver streak. Will and Jim remove the mark, and then Will tricks her into following him to an abandoned house, where he punctures her balloon. After Mr. Dark captures the boys, the Dust Witch puts them under Dark's power. She also attempts to murder Charles but is foiled by his laughter. She is later killed by Charles with a fake bullet upon which he has carved a smile.

The Dwarf

See Tom Fury

Mr. Electrico

See Mr. Cooger

Miss Foley

With a name that strikingly resembles the word "folly," Miss Foley is the boys' seventh-grade teacher. She realizes that Robert is not really her nephew, but she is so enthralled by the carnival that she does not care. When Robert frames the boys for attempting to steal Miss Foley's jewelry, Miss Foley persists in the ruse. She realizes that she must get rid of the meddlesome boys in order to find out what the carnival has to offer her. Later, Miss Foley appears as a little girl, crying over what she has done. The boys try to help her, but she disappears, never to be heard from or seen again. It is presumed that she has been forced into serving the carnival, perhaps transformed into a sideshow freak as well.

Tom Fury

Acting as the harbinger of the coming carnival, Tom Fury, the traveling lightning rod salesman, gives Jim a lightning rod because he senses that the house will be hit by lightning. It is, but only in a metaphorical sense. Tom Fury is enchanted by the storefront display claiming to house "THE MOST BEAUTIFUL WOMAN IN THE WORLD." Tom does indeed see a woman in the ice-block display, though Charles, who had viewed the display earlier, did not. The salesman enters the store with the intent to free the illusory woman by melting the ice, but it appears that, as a consequence, he is transformed into a sideshow freak, the Dwarf. The novel indicates that the Dwarf is a physical manifestation of Tom Fury's flaws, particularly his habitual shirking of responsibility. Throughout his life, Tom Fury has always, and literally, fled before the storm.

Charles William Halloway

Somewhat old to be the father of a young son, Charles Halloway works as a janitor at the library. He tends to work late and lose himself in books. Charles is also saddened by his old age; he feels unable to play with or relate to his son on account of it. When Will is in trouble, however, Charles does everything he can to help, learning how to accept himself, and all of the world, in the process. Charles also comes to know the nature of good and evil. He is the most dynamic of the book's protagonists and is perhaps the most heroic as well.

William Halloway

Will is a light-haired and sweet-natured boy, the foil to his darker counterpart and best friend Jim. Will's experiences fighting the carnival make him more brave and independent, as when he sneaks out alone for the first time in order to trick the Dust Witch. Will wants only to do the right thing and to protect his friend Jim from himself, even when Jim does not necessarily want to be protected. Will comes of age over the course of the novel, growing braver, stronger, and wiser. He also becomes closer to his father, whom he grows to love and respect in a more immediate way than before. By the end of the novel, he is able to recognize the true nature of evil, and he is charged by his father with constantly being on the lookout for it.

The Illustrated Man

See Mr. Dark

Jed

See Mr. Dark

Jim's Mother

Either a widow or a divorce' e (it is unclear which), Jim's mother raises Jim on her own. She is afraid of him leaving her. She feels that once Jim leaves, his father will have fully left as well.

James Nightshade

Will's dark-haired counterpart, Jim is constantly described as being intimately acquainted with the murkier aspects of life (and has a last name signaling as much). He persuades Will to spy on the carnival and is thus ultimately responsible for the consequences that ensue. Jim wants to grow older on the carousel, and he persists in this desire even after he begins to understand Mr. Dark's and the carnival's true nature. Indeed, even after seeing what has happened to Miss Foley and being kidnapped by Dark, Jim still jumps onto the carousel. Yet, emotionally torn between his desires to be older and to be Will's friend (mutually exclusive propositions), Jim becomes physically torn between the ride and Will. As a result, he falls down dead—but he is revived by Will and Charles's gaiety.

Robert

See Mr. Cooger

Mr. Tetley

Mr. Tetley is the owner of the cigar store. He hears the faint calliope music on the night carnival arrives. He also sells Charles a cigar, fortuitously causing Charles to stand over the grate under which the boys are hiding. Charles's presence over the grate distracts Mr. Dark. Will's father also uses the cigar smoke to disorient the Dust Witch just as she begins to sense the boys' presence nearby.

Will's Mother

Existing mainly as a counterpoint to her husband, Will's mother is happy where Charles is not. She also senses Will calling for help in the library, but luckily she does not see him or go in, and she thus avoids becoming another of Mr. Dark's victims.

Themes

Transformation and Duality

Transformations in many guises appear throughout *Something Wicked This Way Comes.* Miss Foley becomes a little girl. Mr. Cooger goes from a man to a boy (acting as Robert, Miss Foley's nephew) to an old man. Tom Fury turns into a dwarf. All of the sideshow freaks were once normal people. Yet there are also less literal transformations. Will is occasionally called William or Willy. Jim's full name is James. Charles Halloway is Dad or Mr. Halloway. Indeed, it is almost as if these characters take on different personalities depending upon how they are addressed. The utmost example of this sort of nominal transformation is Mr. Dark, the cruel, evil, but competent carnival master. Mr. Dark is also the Illustrated Man, a carnival freak with mystical tattoos that allow him to control those in his power. At the end of the story, Mr. Dark transforms himself into a small boy named Jed.

Duality, specifically that between good and evil, is inherently connected to the transformations that occur throughout the novel. For instance, the once-good people who are seduced by the evils of the carnival become evil themselves. Jim is constantly fighting his darker nature. Even good transforms itself into evil, at least in the eyes of evil people. This is how laughter and gaiety are used by Charles as a weapon. Charles's laughter shatters the Mirror Maze, and his smile kills the Dust Witch. His gaiety revives Jim from death. Indeed, Charles tells Jed/Mr. Dark that "good to evil seems evil. So I will do only good to you, Jed. I will simply hold you and watch you poison yourself." Charles's loving embrace vanquishes Dark, who falls down dead.

Acceptance

Lack of acceptance, which could reasonably be called despair, lies at the heart of the carnival's success. In turn, acceptance of the world as it is lies at the heart of the carnival's defeat. Miss Foley is unable to accept herself as she is, as she longs to be younger. This inability to accept herself proves her undoing. Miss Foley is transformed into a young girl, and then she is never seen or heard from again; she has presumably become one of the circus freaks. Charles's initial inability to accept his old age prevents him from enjoying his young son or fostering a relationship with him. Indeed, his lack of acceptance has colored all aspects of his life, such as with how he spent most of his youth trying to be good, missing out on truly living in the process. Unable to accept the world for what it is, Charles spends his free time in the library, burying himself in books and avoiding his wife and, especially, his son. By avoiding life as it truly is, Charles refusing to accept the world and his place in it. As a consequence, he is filled with fear and sadness. It is this fear and sadness that makes him vulnerable to Mr. Dark's powers.

Some part of Charles begins to realize this aspect of himself, and when he accepts who he is and the nature of the world in which he lives, he is able to live fully, with joy and without fear. This is why he is able to conquer the witch and Mr. Dark. As Charles's laughter shatters the mirror, he is laughing "because he accepted everything at last … above all himself and all of life." Indeed, Charles "cried out, released." Death is a part of this "everything," and Charles knows that the fear of death is what lies behind the fear of aging. He is able to accept death and laugh in the face of death, ultimately saving Jim's life because of this. Earlier in the novel, Charles tells his son that the only thing that does not make him sad is death because death is the thing that "scares" and "makes everything else sad." In the last chapter, to the contrary, he tells Will that everything is funny, adding, "Death's funny, God damn it!" Indeed, it is only by accepting his age and his mortality that Charles is able to laugh in the face of death, and also in the face of evil. By doing so, he triumphs over both.

Topics for Further Study

- Study the history of carnivals and circuses. Where and how did they start? How did they evolve into what they are today? Give a class presentation on your findings.

- Mr. Dark capitalizes on the desire of the young to be adults and on the desire of the old to be young. Interview some older adults and some of your young peers about their thoughts on aging, asking various questions on the topic. Summarize your findings in a report.

- Imagine that Jim does take a ride on the carousel and grows older. Write a short story about what happens afterward. Is Jim sad or happy about his transformation? Is he able to return home to his mother? Is he able to remain friends with Will? What does he do with himself?

- Do you think Will is the main protagonist of the novel, or could it be Jim or Charles Halloway? Write an essay on the topic, and be sure to use quotes from the novel in support of your thesis.

Style

Characteristic Diction

The term *diction* refers to the specific word choices and style of writing used in a literary work. The diction in *Something Wicked This Way Comes* is very unique, featuring long, choppy sentences and hyberbolic (exaggerated) descriptive language. Indeed, at times, the diction takes on an almost nonsensical feeling. The sentence structure often also becomes somewhat stilted. Take, for instance, the following passage regarding Mr. Dark's tattoos as they disappear: There the obscene wink of the navel eye gasped in on itself, there the nipple-iris of a trumpeting mastodon went blind and raved at its blindness; each and every picture remembered from the tall Mr. Dark now rendered down to miniature canvas pronged and forked over a boy's tennis-racket bones.

Several examples such as this can be found in the novel. Furthermore, it seems that the novel's title is not the only inspiration taken from Shakespeare's *Macbeth*. The diction in *Something Wicked This Way Comes* is highly reminiscent of the play's dialogue, specifically that of the three witches featured in *Macbeth*.

Eye Motifs

A motif is any repetitive literary device, and there are several in *Something Wicked This Way Comes*. One such example is the concept of having an image burned into one's eyes. This concept first appears when Tom Fury explains the effects of being struck by lightning. Tom says, "Any boy hit by lightning, lift his lid and there on his eyeball, pretty as the Lord's Prayer on a pin, find the last scene the boy ever saw!" This conceit is repeated after Jim and Will first witness the transformative powers of the carousel. Will is afraid that Mr. Dark will know what he has seen because it has been burned into his eyes as if he has been struck by lightning. A related motif is that of the eye as a camera. Cooger, disguised as Miss Foley's nephew, takes pictures of the boys with his eyes. The Dwarf does the same when he looks at the grill that Jim and Will are hiding under. Only later, once the Dwarf develops and reviews the so-called pictures, does he realize what he has seen. Other motifs focus on the powers of Dark's illustrations and the nature of good and evil.

The Circus

The circus is believed to have evolved from Greek chariot races. In ancient Rome, chariot races were coupled with horse shows, trained animal acts, and other performances, including juggling and acrobatics. Roman circuses were originally held in stationary buildings. After the fall of Rome, however, individual performers traveled throughout Europe, presenting no more than a few such acts at a time. It is also thought that troupes of Gypsies may have capitalized on circus acts, traveling in large wagon-based caravans and presenting shows from town to town. In this manner, the circus acts traveled to England. By the 1700s, the most popular circus acts in England featured trick horseback riding, and the modern circus ring was developed to accommodate these performances. By the 1790s, the circus had traveled to the United States, and the first circus tent was introduced there in 1825. Another now-definitive circus feature was also developed in America, that of the traveling sideshow, which was first offered by the circus owners P. T. Barnum and William Cameron Coup. Coup was also the first circus manager to use trains as a means of transporting the circus. This method is still used today. A current and still-operating incarnation of the circus founded by P. T. Barnum and William Cameron Coup performs as the

Ringling Bros. and Barnum & Bailey Circus.

The Idyll of the 1950s and Early 1960s

Green Town, the town in which *Something Wicked This Way Comes* is set, reflects the cultural idyll of the 1950s and early 1960s. Traditionally, an idyll is a romanticized version of a rustic setting, such as a work of art portraying a happy shepherd and his flock or the peaceful beauty of nature. The idyll tends to overlook the fact that the shepherd may be cold and hungry, or that the peaceful beauty of nature can easily become a deadly hurricane. America during the 1950s and early 1960s became a sort of cultural idyll in and of itself; that is, the nation mythologized itself as a land of small towns filled with happy families with wholesome values. Cultural images of the happily married housewife, the dapper-suited husband, their smiling children, and their house with a green lawn and a white picket fence abounded. Popular television shows such as *Leave It to Beaver* (1957-1963) perpetuated these images and their corresponding myths of happiness in conformity.

Compare & Contrast

- **1960s:** The average life expectancy for males in the United States is around sixty-six years. Thus, at the age of fifty-four, Charles Halloway is indeed an old man, or close to it.

Today: The average life expectancy for males in the United States is around seventy-five years. A fifty-four-year-old man would not be considered old but would instead be seen as middle-aged.

- **1960s:** It is common for children, especially boys, to go into town unaccompanied by adults, just as Will and Jim do in the story.

Today: Children, especially those in urban areas, are less and less likely to be unaccompanied by an adult. Widespread fear of sexual predators is largely the cause of this phenomenon.

- **1960s:** Traveling circuses such as the one portrayed in the novel are just beginning to lose the popularity that they have enjoyed. This is due to the rise of entertainment in the form of television and movies.

Today: Traveling circuses still exist, though most of the smaller companies have long since folded. The circus has made a resurgence in a reinvented form as "highbrow" entertainment, as evidenced by the success of the highly artistic (and animal-and sideshow-free) Cirque du Soleil.

Indeed, many Americans were content to perceive their nation as a happy and wholesome place, something like Green Town, with children running safely through the town, moms staying home to cook, dads going off to work, and townspeople attending church on Sunday. In the novel, Will and Jim know the shopkeepers by name, and they know where their schoolteacher lives. Yet, just as the carnival reveals (and exploits) the dark underbelly of the town, its people, and their desires, so, too, does a closer look at the era that valued "mom and apple pie" above all else reveal that underbelly. For instance, outside of marriage, women had little opportunity. They had few career options aside from that of homemaker, and even if they did work, they were paid pennies on the dollar when compared to their male counterparts. Racial segregation was still legal in the United States, and racism was a culturally acceptable aspect of daily life. Censorship was also enforced via stringent obscenity laws. Bradbury's carnival, like the time in which it is set, appears innocent, but it is altogether something else entirely. Indeed, by the late 1960s, a countercultural movement—with unprecedented (before or since) power—was in full swing. Along these lines, *Something Wicked This Way Comes* can be read as a commentary on the social idyll of the time in which it was written and published.

Critical Overview

Though Ray Bradbury's oeuvre in its entirety is valued as a major and course-changing contribution to genre writing and American fiction, critics often find fault with his individual publications. Indeed, *Something Wicked This Way Comes* was not initially well received, yet it has remained in print for more than forty years. It is also known as one of the best works by one of America's best-known writers. The contradiction is a confusing one. For instance, Gary K. Wolfe, writing in the *Dictionary of Literary Biography*, notes, "Despite the occasional power generated by the sheer wealth of invention in *Something Wicked This Way Comes*, the work failed to establish Bradbury as a significant novelist, and Bradbury began to focus more and more on dramatic writing." (Indeed, *Something Wicked This Way Comes* was originally conceived as a screenplay.) Wolfe also states that "the novel suffers from an artificially inflated style and a barely controlled wealth of imagery and incident."

Steven Dimeo, in an essay in the *Journal of Popular Culture*, remarks, "At his worst, Bradbury has belabored morality to death. Charles Halloway, who discourses lengthily on Good and Evil in *Something Wicked*, epitomizes this self-conscious moralizing." Yet, more benevolent reviewers have found much of value in the book. Anita T. Sullivan, writing in the *English Journal*, calls the novel

Bradbury's "finest work of fantasy," adding that it "is a good example of the fusion of fantasy, horror, and nostalgia which he manages so well." Despite the range of critical opinion, thus far *Something Wicked This Way Comes* has withstood the test of time, a feat that is rarely accomplished even by books that are universally acclaimed.

What Do I Read Next?

- William Shakespeare's play *Macbeth* (c. 1606) contains the quote from which the title of *Something Wicked This Way Comes* is taken. While the play has a very different storyline, the two works share similar themes.

- Another classic Bradbury novel is *The Martian Chronicles* (1950), which portrays earthlings as they colonize Mars and eradicate the Martians.

- *Wild, Weird, and Wonderful: The American Circus 1901-1927, as Seen by F. W. Glasier, Photographer* (2003) is a collection of photographs of circus acts from the time that inspired the carnival attractions presented in *Something Wicked This Way Comes*.

- Stephen King's *Needful Things* (1991) is an homage to *Something Wicked This Way Comes*. The novel features a shopkeeper, Gaunt, who somehow manages to offer products that speak to the townspeople's innermost desires. Like Miss Foley, however, Gaunt's customers soon become ensnared by an evil puppet master.

Sources

Arias, Elizabeth, "United States Life Tables, 2004," in *National Vital Statistics Reports*, Vol. 56, No. 9, December 28, 2007.

Bradbury, Ray, "In His Words," Web site of Ray Bradbury, http://www.raybradbury.com/inhiswords02.html (accessed July 7, 2008).

———, *Something Wicked This Way Comes*, Avon, 1998.

Central Intelligence Agency, *World Factbook*, s.v. "United States," http://www.cia.gov/library/publications/the-worldfactbook/geos/us.html (accessed July 31, 2008).

"The Circus in America: 1793-1940," http://www.circusinamerica.org/public/ (accessed July 31, 2008).

Dimeo, Steven, "Man and Apollo: Religion in Bradbury's Science Fiction," in *Short Story Criticism*, Vol. 53, The Gale Group, 2002; originally published in *Journal of Popular Culture*, Vol. 5, No. 4, Spring 1972, pp. 970-78.

Sullivan, Anita T., "Ray Bradbury and Fantasy," in *English Journal*, Vol. 61, No. 9, December 1972, pp. 1309-14.

Wolfe, Gary K., "Ray Bradbury," in *Dictionary of*

Literary Biography, Vol. 8, *Twentieth-Century American Science-Fiction Writers*, Gale Group, 1989, pp. 16-33.

Further Reading

Aggelis, Steven L., ed., *Conversations with Ray Bradbury*, University Press of Mississippi, 2004.

> This collection of interviews with Bradbury provides much insight into the life and work of a man whose stories shaped the genre of science fiction.

Arbus, Diane, *Diane Arbus: Revelations*, Random House, 2003.

> Arbus was a renowned photographer who achieved fame for her images of circus freaks and other bizarre personages. Notably, her photographs were produced during the same period in which *Something Wicked This Way Comes* was written.

Eller, Jonathan R., and William F. Touponce, *Ray Bradbury: The Life of Fiction*, Kent State University Press, 2004.

> Eller and Touponce's biography is one of the most comprehensive available. It sheds much light on Bradbury's early career as a publisher of pulp fiction, an avocation that largely influenced the author's developing writing style.

Hartzman, Marc, *American Sideshow: An Encyclopedia of History's Most Wondrous and Curiously Strange Performers*, Jeremy P. Tarcher/Penguin, 2005.

This academic overview of sideshow acts and circus freaks grounds the fantastical figures in *Something Wicked This Way Comes* in historical fact.

9 781375 401272